Tadpole Books are published by Jump!, 5357 Penn Avenue South, Minneapolis, MN 55419, www.jumplibrary.com

Copyright ©2020 Jump. International copyright reserved in all countries. No part of this book may be reproduced in any form without written permission from the publisher.

Editor: Jenna Trnka **Designer:** Anna Peterson **Translator:** Annette Granat

Photo Credits: Dorling Kindersley ltd/Alamy, cover; Melinda Fawver/Shutterstock, 1; Anthony Aneese Totah Jr/Dreamstime, 2tl, 3; Ra\'id Khalil/Dreamstime, 2br, 4–5; Jay Ondreicka/Shutterstock, 2ml, 6–7; Ekaterina Staats/Dreamstime, 2tr, 8–9; Minden Pictures/SuperStock, 2bl, 10–11; John Sterrett/Dreamstime, 2mr, 12–13; Alexander Sviridov/Shutterstock, 14–15; Psycnotic Nature/Shutterstock, 16.

Library of Congress Cataloging-in-Publication Data
Names: Nilsen, Genevieve, author.
Title: Las serpientes / por Genevieve Nilsen.
Other titles: Snakes. Spanish
Description: Tadpole books edition. | Minneapolis: Jump!, Inc., (2020) | Series: Animales en tu jardín | Includes index. | Audience: Ages 3–6
Identifiers: LCCN 2019042898 (print) | LCCN 2019042899 (ebook) | ISBN 9781645272649 (hardcover) | ISBN 9781645272656 (paperback)
ISBN 9781645272663 (ebook)
Subjects: LCSH: Snakes—Juvenile literature.
Classification: LCC QL666.O6 N5518 2020 (print) | LCC QL666.O6 (ebook) | DDC 597.96—dc23

ANIMALES EN TU JARDÍN

LAS SERPIENTES

por Genevieve Nilsen

TABLA DE CONTENIDO

Palabras a saber.........................2

Las serpientes..........................3

¡Repasemos!............................16

Índice..................................16

tadpole
en español

PALABRAS A SABER

amarillas

anaranjadas

azules

grises

rojas

verdes

LAS SERPIENTES

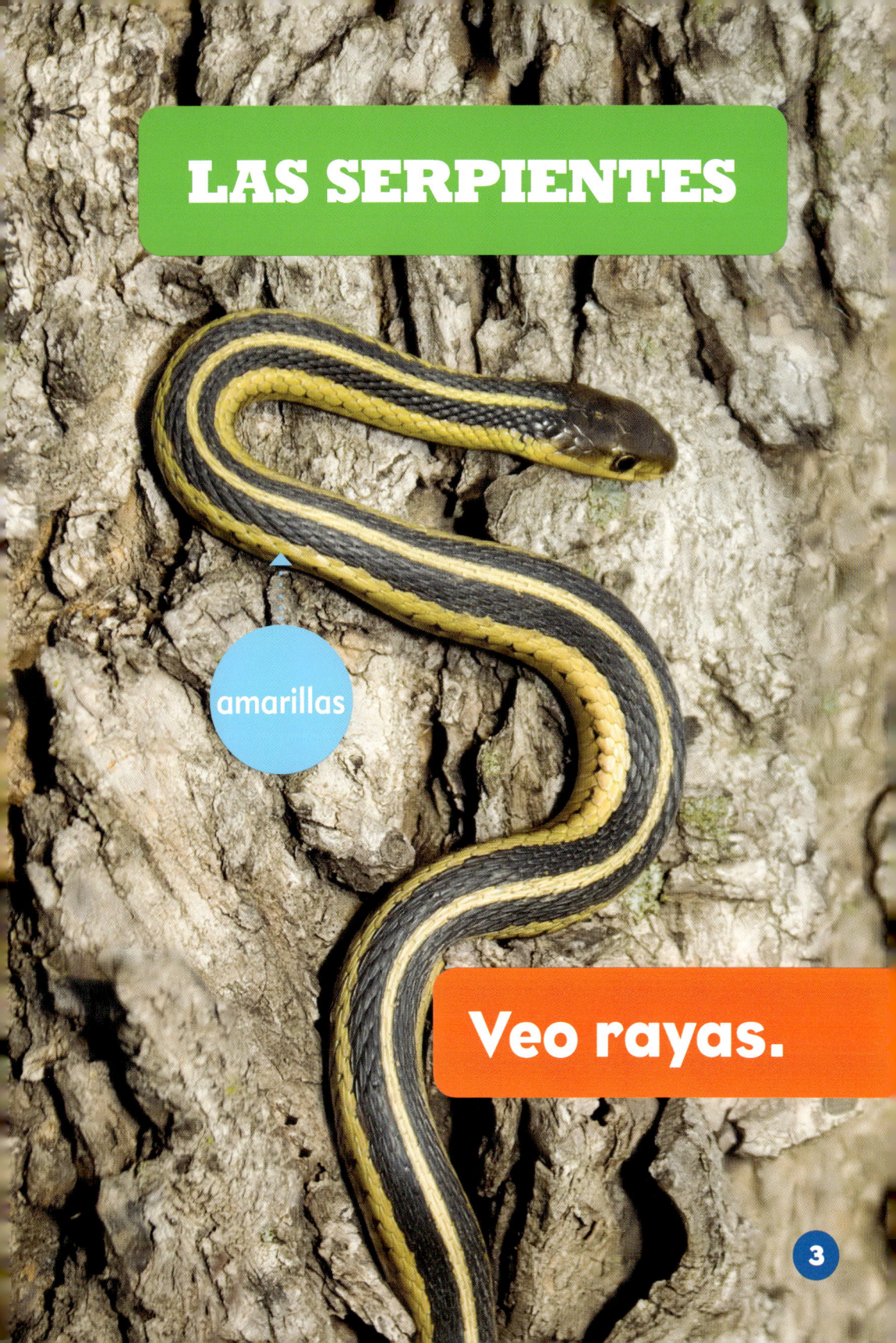

amarillas

Veo rayas.

verdes

Veo rayas.

Veo rayas.

anaranjadas

Veo rayas.

rojas

Veo rayas.

grises

Veo rayas.

blancas

Veo rayas.

¡REPASEMOS!

No todas las serpientes de jardín tienen rayas. ¿De qué color es esta serpiente?

ÍNDICE

amarillas 3
anaranjadas 8
azules 6
blancas 14
grises 12
rayas 3, 5, 7, 9, 11, 13, 15
rojas 10
verdes 4